MADE T

Going Through the Process

A 12 Day Devotional & Journal

Eve "Starr" Geiggar

Going Through the Process
Made to Manifest Series

Authors: Eve "Starr" Geiggar
Publication Services – Kingdom News Publication Services, LLC.

DISCLAIMER

Printed in the United States of America.
ISBN 978-1735362090

KINGDOM NEWS TODAY
Publication Services, LLC

Dedication

This journal is dedicated to men and women who has gone through life struggles and didn't think they would come out of it. But not only did you come out, God brought you out better mentally, better physically and better spiritually. That is why I dedicate this journal to you. May God continue to enrich you and manifest you.

I pray this journal will bless you and allow you to know, you are not alone and you will come out victorious. Stay the course and stay connected to God!!

Table of Contents

Lord, You have chosen me for a time such as this to go through the process to be made manifest. To write, seek Your face and pray. That Oh Lord I will do!

While going through the process God made me to Manifest

MADE TO

Manifest

Luke 8:17

Day 1

Lord, It's Me

Lord,

I want to be a better me today! Spiritual, Naturally, and Physically! I want Your Spirit to dwell in me. Help me not to get caught upon the pleasing of people that I miss out on You and not pleasing You. God, I need Your help today. I need Your discernment today. I want to know what pleases You. I want to know when, where and how to go and what to do to be in Your will. Lord, help me know how to do whatever it is that pleases You! Lord, I am stuck and I feel lost. Help me today. If not, I do not know what I will do. I long to be in Your presence, effective in the Kingdom but right now I feel so torn. Why is it I look for validation and approval from everyone except from You? Oh Lord, please come at once, affirm me, come to my rescue quickly.

Lord, help me to relinquish myself, sit down, and get out of self. Tame my thoughts so I can hear You. I understand it is for a purpose that I go through and come out as pure gold.

Lord, you told me through Your word, to *"Trust in You with all my heart, mind, body, and soul and lean not to my own understanding, in all I do acknowledge You and You will give me strength, security and joy. You will direct my path"* (Proverbs 3:5-6).

> *"I can do all things [which He has called me to do] through Him who strengthens and empowers me [to fulfill His purpose—I am self-sufficient in Christ's sufficiency; I am ready for anything and equal to anything through Him who infuses me with inner strength and confident peace.] Nevertheless, it was right of you to share [with me] in my difficulties. And you Philippians know that in the early days of preaching the gospel, after I left Macedonia, no church shared with me in the matter of giving and receiving except you alone; for even in Thessalonica, you sent a gift more than once for my needs. Not that I seek the gift itself, but I do seek the profit which increases to your [heavenly] account [the blessing which is accumulating for you]. But I have received everything in full and more; I am amply supplied, having received from Epaphroditus the gifts you sent me. They are the fragrant aroma of an offering, an acceptable*

2

sacrifice which God welcomes and in which He delights." Philippians 4:13-18 AMP

As you go through life's struggles, trust that God is working it out for you and through you for a greater purpose. Stay connected to God!

Questions to Ponder

Why is it so hard for you to trust God, while going through?

_____

_____

_____

_____

_____

_____

_____

_____

_____

_____

_____

_____

Day 2

The Mirror That Reflects Me

Lord,

Today is no different than yesterday, but today I have realized I have fallen for the tricks, the lies, and the deceit that the devil has spoken in my ear. Oh Lord, I need help and I need it now! I am drowning from all this negativity I believed for so long about who I was or even who I am now. There must be a way out, Lord I know You are speaking, but I cannot hear. Let me out of here I need You. Please come in a hurry, Oh Lord.

> *"The LORD is good to those who wait [confidently] for Him, to those who seek Him [on the authority of God's word]."* Lamentations 3:25 AMP

"Therefore, do not be foolish and thoughtless, but understand and firmly grasp what the will of the Lord is." Ephesians 5:17 AMP

"I will come with the mighty acts of the Lord GOD [and in His strength]; I will make mention of Your righteousness, Yours alone." Psalms 71:16 AMP

"The LORD is my strength and my [impenetrable] shield; My heart trusts [with unwavering confidence] in Him, and I am helped; Therefore, my heart greatly rejoices, and with my song I shall thank Him and praise Him." Psalms 28:7 AMP

"And now there remain faith [abiding trust in God and His promises], hope [confident expectation of eternal salvation], love [unselfish love for others growing out of God's love for me], these three [the choicest graces]; but the greatest of these is love." 1 Corinthians 13:13 AMP

In the process God is always near, all you must do is trust and rely on Him! I promise you; He is speaking… but are you listening.

Questions to Ponder

Am I actively listening to the voice of God?

_____

_____

Day 3

I Must Live a Righteous Life

Righteous: Right with God!

By faith I am made righteous with You.

> *"But without faith it is impossible for me to [walk with God and] please Him, for whoever comes [near] to God must [necessarily] believe that God exists and that He rewards those who [earnestly and diligently] seek Him." Hebrews 11:6 AMP*

Lord,

My heart sings, "Open the eyes of my heart Lord! I want to see you. David wrote in Psalms 119:18 AMP, *"Open my eyes [to spiritual truth] so that I may behold Wonderful things from Your law."* Today is a new day! New mercies and New Grace!

I am not the same as days before, I feel You, oh Lord. There is a shifting taking place. Lord, help me to be in position. I have been bought for a price paid for by Your blood. I must live a righteous life because my life is no longer my own, but Yours, Oh Lord. I am redeemed by the blood of the Lamb and I have been set free.

> *"The LORD your God is in your midst, A Warrior who saves. He will rejoice over you with joy; He will be quiet in His love [making no mention of your past sins], He will rejoice over you with shouts of joy." Zephaniah 3:17 AMP*

> *"Do you not know that your body is a temple of the Holy Spirit who is within you, whom you have [received as a gift] from God, and that you are not your own [property]?" 1 Corinthians 6:19*

Faith is trusting God to be Faithful.

Questions to Ponder

Are you trusting God to be Faithful? What are your eyes fixed on? Are you allowing the righteousness of God to fill your temple?

_____

_____

Day 4

Remaining Still

"Be still and know (recognize, understand) that I am God. I will be exalted among the nations! I will be exalted in the earth." Psalm 46:10 AMP

Lord,

You often tell me to be still and know You are God. I know that You are God, I know this. Yet, I find it to be hard and difficult for me to remain still because I want what I want. Help me to identify what is causing me to not be still. Help me to identify what causes me to be stressed and tense, show me what I need to do to let go. Lord, I pray for stillness in my spirit through You.

I need your help. Help me address the root cause of this mess that I have held onto. Help me to embrace You and the power of being still.

> *"So will My word be which goes out of My mouth; It will not return to Me void (useless, without result), Without accomplishing what I desire, and without succeeding in the matter for which I sent it." Isaiah 55:11 AMP*

> *"A man's mind plans his way [as he journeys through life], But the LORD directs his steps and establishes them." Proverbs 16:9 AMP*

> *"Be still and know (recognize, understand) that I am God. I will be exalted among the nations! I will be exalted in the earth." Psalm 46:10 AMP*

Questions to Ponder

Amid your trials and tribulations, are you being still and waiting on God?

_____

_____

_____

_____

_____

_____

Day 5

Help!

Lord,

Please help, it is like I take one step forward only to take two back. Help me! I beg of You. I ask you to manage my feelings and to manage my emotions. Lord, give me wisdom instead of trusting my feelings. I no longer want to operate in my own strength, but I know I need Your strength and assistance.

I have been assigned this process and I desire to come through it, but I can only do it with Your help. Lord I need Your help, I do not like what I am feeling. What is really going on? I chose to trust You.

Some days will feel just like this and your thoughts will be all over the place, but we have a choice to put our trust in God. You chose, feelings come and go but the word of God remains.

"No temptation [regardless of its source] has overtaken or enticed you that is not common to human experience [nor is any temptation unusual or beyond human resistance]; but God is faithful [to His word—He is compassionate and trustworthy], and He will not let you be tempted beyond your ability [to resist], but along with the temptation He [has in the past and is now and] will [always] provide the way out as well, so that you will be able to endure it [without yielding, and will overcome temptation with joy]." 1 Corinthians 10:13 AMP

"When I am afraid, I will put my trust and faith in You." Psalm 56:3 AMP

"Commit your way to the Lord; Trust in Him also and He will do it." Psalm 37:5 AMP

Questions to Ponder

What is your driving force; feelings or trust? What are some of the things you need to gain control over?

_____

_____

Day 6

Rest, Relax and Renounce

Lord,

This is truly the day You have made, and I chose to rejoice and be glad in You! Today I choose to rest, relax, and renounce.

For as long as I can remember oh Lord, I stopped relaxing. Instead, I built walls up to make me look strong, but in reality, I was weak. I wanted to be something I was not to make people think I was more than I really was. I lost who I was and have not been able to rest or relax peacefully. This has led me to wanting to be in control of the things in my life. Fear gripped my life and I began pleasing people and became entangled with those who did not even like me.

I have realized that I have been standing in the gap for others, asking You to heal and restore everyone except for me. But today, I'm asking You Lord, to heal and restore me. I need your healing; I want to be healed and whole in You. In order for me to be that go-to person everyone expects me to be, I need to be healed and whole in You. When others come to me, I will remove self out the way and I promise I will point them to You.

I now realized that I wanted to be liked and thought highly of, but now I just want You. Oh Lord, what do I do. I refuse to be that person of my past. My ears are tuned to Your voice and I heard a still small but powerful voice say, *"Renounce it, let go of all past failures, all the negative thinking that tells you, I am not good enough, I am not worthy enough. Let go of people pleasing and always trying to fit in and being validated. Acknowledge your shortcoming and truly allow Me to heal you. No more limitations, but walking in my newness and embracing what it really means to relax, rest and renounce so you can hear me when I speak to you."*

"For I know the plans and thoughts that I have for you,' says the LORD, 'plans for peace and well-being and not for disaster, to give you a future and a hope." Jeremiah 29:11 AMP

And Lord, when it seems I am heading back to who I once was, please remind me not to lose focus, renounce it and know I am Yours

Questions to Ponder

What do you need to renounce?

_____

_____

_____

_____

_____

_____

_____

_____

_____

_____

_____

_____

_____

_____

_____

_____

_____

Day 7

The Vow

Lord,

Today I make a new vow with You. I am reminded of the vow I made to you over eleven year ago when I said, *"If you keep me, I will keep You and even when it seems I do not want to be kept, Lord, please keep me."* Today's vow is a vow to serve, *"I vow to serve You wholehearted with no reservation. I will serve You, live for You, and do whatever I need to do in the Kingdom for You."*

For when I was broken, and a mess and You saved me. You got this, no need for me to help. All I must do is stand still and watch You work. My spirit is broken and I have renounced all that is in me that is not of You, I repent of the things that have kept me from you and desire to walk in Your righteousness.

"Do not be hasty with your mouth [speaking careless words or vows] or impulsive in thought to bring up a matter before God. For God is in heaven and you are on earth; therefore let your words be few. For the dream comes through much effort, and the voice of the fool through many words. When you make a vow or a pledge to God, do not put off paying it; for God takes no pleasure in fools [who thoughtlessly mock Him]. Pay what you vow. It is better that you should not vow than that you should vow and not pay. Do not allow your speech to cause you to sin, and do not say before the messenger (priest) of God that it was a mistake. Why should God be angry because of your voice (words) and destroy the work of your hands? For in a multitude of dreams and in a flood of words there is worthlessness. Rather [reverently] fear God [and worship Him with awe-filled respect, knowing who He is]." Ecclesiastes 5:2-7 AMP

"For [godly] sorrow that is in accord with the will of God produces a repentance without regret, leading to salvation; but worldly sorrow [the hopeless sorrow of those who do not believe] produces death." 2 Corinthians 7:10 AMP

Questions to Ponder

What is your vow to God?

_____

_____

_____

_____

_____

_____

_____

_____

_____

_____

_____

_____

_____

_____

_____

_____

Day 8

Moving Forward, Never Looking Back

Lord,

I cannot go back to who I used to be; broken, people pleasing, living in fear and turmoil. I know You have redeemed me and delivered me. I thank You for Your son Jesus and the work He did on the cross on my behalf. I am no longer the same and I have been changed.

Lord, I need Your help! For it seems to be easier to go back than to move forward. I am reminded of Romans 8:28, where all things work together for the good of those who love You. I am determined not to go back, but move forward in You. Help me to embrace Your will. Allow me to bind and rebuke every tactic the enemy, Satan himself brings to me that tries to kill, steal and destroy my destiny in You. I refuse to miss You, Lord.

No more boundaries, no more reservations, no more limits and no more excuses, for You are the source and the supplier of all my needs. I trust You God for what You are doing and what You are going to do in my life. I am Your vessel, a soldier in the Army of the Lord and I will no longer look back, but will turn and move forward in You. I will no longer live beneath my spiritual, natural, physical means, for in You, I have all things.

I serve a God who is more than capable of keeping His Promises.

"And we know [with great confidence] that God [who is deeply concerned about us] causes all things to work together [as a plan] for good for those who love God, to those who are called according to His plan and purpose." Romans 8:28 AMP

"The thief comes only to steal and kill and destroy. I came that they may have and enjoy life, and have it in abundance [to the full, till it overflows]." John 10:10 AMP

"And my God will liberally supply (fill until full) your every need according to His riches in glory in Christ Jesus." Philippians 4:19 AMP

"Ask and keep on asking and it will be given to you; seek and keep on seeking and you will find; knock

and keep on knocking and the door will be opened to you." Matthew 7:7 AMP

Questions to Ponder

What steps are you taking, to stay on the right path? What are some of those things you need to leave in the past? Are you beginning to see a brighter future in Him?

_____

_____

_____

_____

_____

_____

_____

_____

_____

_____

_____

_____

_____

_____

Day 9

Change

Lord,

The word for me today is Change.

Change has been defined as to make or become different. I am not sure how You have changed me but, Lord, I know I have been changed. Lord, it is like a dawn of a new day. My perception has changed, my thought process has changed, how I view myself and others has changed. I am no longer bound with chains; I am free all because of You. I have been released.

Oh Lord, just like a caterpillar goes through the metamorphosis stage to be changed or transformed into a beautiful butterfly. You, Oh Lord have transformed me.

Oh Lord, I cannot wait to see what I will come out to be.

"I am convinced and confident of this very thing, that He who has begun a good work in you will [continue to] perfect and complete it until the day of Christ Jesus [the time of His return]." Philippians 1:6 AMP

"And do not be conformed to this world [any longer with its superficial values and customs] but be [a]transformed and progressively changed [as you mature spiritually] by the renewing of your mind [focusing on godly values and ethical attitudes], so that you may prove [for yourselves] what the will of God is, that which is good and acceptable and perfect [in His plan and purpose for you]." Romans 12:2 AMP

"Create in me a clean heart, O God, and renew a right and steadfast spirit within me. Do not cast me away from Your presence and do not take Your Holy Spirit from me." Psalm 51:10-12 AMP

Restore to me the joy of Your salvation and sustain me with a willing spirit.

Questions to Ponder

What will it take for you to Change? What changes have you already seen in your life? Are you willing to Change?

_____

_____

_____

_____

_____

_____

_____

_____

_____

_____

_____

_____

_____

_____

_____

_____

_____

Day 10

Identifying Things that Keep Me Bound

Lord,

Today is a great day to write out my fears, worries and doubts. I struggled with the fear of failure, not being enough. The fear of dying, my family or loved ones dying. The fear of not being in control, losing my job, not being accepted. The fear of intimidation. The fear of totally letting go and truly allowing You to have Your way, in my heart. The fear of not being loved. The fear of not being in Your will. The fear of not filling my purpose and plan You have for me. The fear of hearing, but not listening to You. The fear of letting You down, Lord. The fear of being struck and going back to where I used to be before You delivered me, Oh Lord. The fear of forgetting.

The fear of sickness and the fear of what people will say about me.

Oh Lord, I feared so long of not being in Your will until I was disobedient because I allowed fear to cripple me in my walk with You. But You said in 1 John 4:18, *"There is no fear in love [dread does not exist]. But perfect (complete, full-grown) love drives out fear, because fear involves [the expectation of divine] punishment, so the one who is afraid [of God's judgment] is not perfected in love [has not grown into a sufficient understanding of God's love]."* I am free!!! Lord, You are so much BIGGER than my fears, intimidations or even foes. Today I write them down as a sign of me giving my fears to You.

> *"Trying to learn [by experience] what is pleasing to the Lord [and letting your lifestyles be examples of what is most acceptable to Him—your behavior expressing gratitude to God for your salvation]."* Ephesians 5:10 AMP

> *"Let his flesh be restored and become fresher than in youth. Let him return to the days of his youthful strength."* Job 33:25 AMP

Release every fear that weighs you down today. So that you too can be free in your mind and move forward in your purpose and destiny.

Questions to Ponder

What has kept you bound?

_____

_____

_____

_____

_____

_____

_____

_____

_____

_____

_____

_____

_____

_____

_____

Day 11

Reminder

Lord,

Today I write scriptures to encourage me, I am designed to go through the process. My trust and hope are in You, Oh Lord!!

> *"Behold, God, my salvation! I will trust and not be afraid, For the Lord God is my strength and song. Yes, He has become my salvation." Isaiah 12:2 AMP*

> *"Jesus Christ is [eternally changeless, always] the same yesterday and today and forever." Hebrew 13:8 AMP*

"Peace I leave with you; My [perfect] peace I give to you; not as the world gives do I give to you. Do not let your heart be troubled, nor let it be afraid. [Let My perfect peace calms you in every circumstance and give you courage and strength for every challenge.]" John 14:27 AMP

"I have told you these things, so that in Me you may have [perfect] peace. In the world you have tribulation and distress and suffering, but be courageous [be confident, be undaunted, be filled with joy]; I have overcome the world." [My conquest is accomplished, My victory abiding.]" John 16:33 AMP

"And the peace of God [that peace which reassures the heart, that peace] which transcends all understanding, [that peace which] stands guard over your hearts and your minds in Christ Jesus [is yours]." Philippians 4:7 AMP

I serve a God who not only encourages me to believe, but to believe mountain sized BIG!!!

Questions to Ponder

Think BIG!!! What are you believing God to do in your life? What is your mountain size BIG?

_____

_____

Day 12

Made to Manifest

Lord,

You are awesome!!! Oh, how I Praise and Worship Your Name through this process of healing and becoming whole. Oh Lord, You spoke a word and birth something new in me. You spoke and said Made to Manifest (I made you, to Manifest). To be made visible.

You made me, Oh Lord!!!

Never underestimate the power of the process and going through. In those times, God speaks and birth new things in us and through us for the Kingdom of God. For us to fulfill His purpose and plan.

"For there is nothing hidden that will not become evident, nor anything secret that will not be known and come out into the open." Luke 8:17 AMP

Allow God to make you Manifest!!!

Questions to Ponder

How do you see yourself? What is God manifesting in you for His Kingdom?

_____

_____

_____

_____

_____

_____

_____

_____

_____

_____

_____

_____

_____

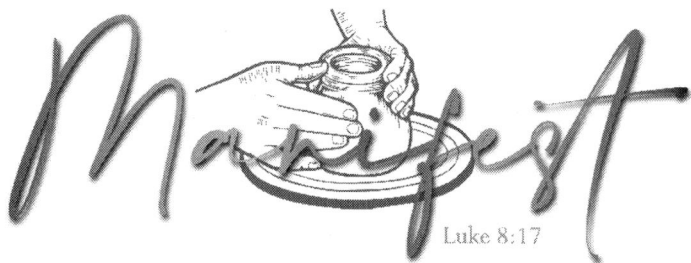

MADE TO

Manifest

Luke 8:17

Made in the USA
Las Vegas, NV
15 April 2021

21514192R00044